SAVE AMERICA

ONLY CHRISTIANS CAN DO IT

ETHAN GRAHAM

BIG REFLECTION BOOKS

II

Save America: Only Christians Can Do It
Text and Illustration Copyright © 2020 Big Reflection Books, LLC
Cover by: Big Reflection Books Design Department
Editor: Charles Richards
Save America: Only Christians Can Do It © 2020 Big Reflection Books, LLC
All rights reserved. Published by Big Reflection Books, LLC.

All rights reserved. Published by Big Reflection Books, LLC. No part of this book may be reproduced in any form by any electronic or mechanical means including photocopying, recording, or information storage and retrieval without permission in writing from the publisher Big Reflection Books, LLC —except in the case of a brief quotation (up to 50 words) embodied in a media article, broadcast, or a book review. For all permissions please contact Big Reflection Books, LLC, Attention: Permission Department, P.O. Box 904, Flagler Beach, FL 32136 USA or publicity@bigreflectionbooks.com. Please be aware of the fact that if you purchase this book without a cover it is 'stolen property.' If this book is sold without a cover, it is a 'stripped book.' This means that this book was reported as unsold, or destroyed, to the publisher. Selling a stripped book is illegal. Thank you for protecting the rights of the author and publisher.

Save America: Only Christians Can Do It is a work of fiction. The views expressed in this book belong to the author alone; not Big Reflection Books, LLC or our staff. If the content of this book bothers, offends, or upsets you in any way, then stop reading it. It's impossible to make every reader of a book feel happy and validated, and this book is no different. Therefore, use your own sound judgment when you make the decision to read, or allow your children to read, the content of this book, and you accept the fact that Big Reflection Books, LLC and the author are not legally responsible if, for what ever reason, you, the reader, don't like the content of this book.

Print ISBN: 978-1-945463-90-7
Digital ISBN: 978-1-945463-58-7
www.bigreflectionbooks.com
Printed in Lavergne, TN United States of America
First Edition 2021

Print Edition

    1 2 3 4 5 6 7 8 9 10 11   JIL/GIL   15 18 11 71

CONTENTS

1 Who Am I?

3 Police

9 Do All Lives Matter?

13 Changing the Laws

21 Who Is the Enemy?

39 Was This Day Foretold?

53 What Does It All Mean?

61 Slavery…Let's Go There

79 America Only Has One Way Out

101 Bibliography

Save America: Only Christians Can Do It

Who Am I?

I grew up in a racially diverse neighborhood. I have seen and experienced racism on all sides. My DNA shows lineage from Africa, Europe, Asia, Middle East, South America, and some Native American.

My family has black and white members. I thought I was an American, but now there is a narrative being pushed that I have to be Black, White, Asian,

Native American, Latino, rich, poor, Democrat, Republican, conservative, liberal, blue-collar, white-collar, young, old, privileged, underprivileged, racist, non-racist, and the labels grow every day.

I must be judged for a history that I was not alive to witness. I should become what a group says I must be based on what labels are placed upon me. They say I have no choice. I am constantly being told I have to adjust and contort myself into a box that fits all the labels that are being forced upon me.

These labels define who I am, despite the fact I scream I am not what these labels claim. I did not choose these labels. The propaganda machine chose them for me. I have only chosen one label in my life, and that is a Christian. They are beginning to say I cannot have that label anymore.

Police

I have friends and family members in law enforcement. I also have friends and family that have been arrested for various crimes (mostly drugs). I have a family member that has been in and out of prison their entire life. They are currently in prison, and will remain in there until they die.

I've been pulled over by the cops

several times. More than I care to admit. I once got pulled over for flashing my headlights. Apparently, it is illegal to flash your lights in my state to warn fellow drivers that the police are up the road with a radar gun. I'm sure you're laughing right now. Yes. I did get pulled over for that.

I waited until I was out of sight to flash my lights, but there was a motorcycle cop. I did not see him coming towards me on the other side of the road. He was probably a runner returning to home base.

I pulled over as I was instructed. I parked the car and turned off the engine. I rolled the window down halfway, and I placed my hands on the steering wheel in the 10/2 position.

The officer came up to the car with his hand on his gun holster—for his protection in case I had a weapon. I understand this. I told you I have friends and family and law enforcement.

My dog popped his head out the back window to say hello. There was no growling from my dog. He was probably hoping to get a treat. However, the officer asked me to roll the window up, so the dog would be contained in the backseat of the car. I did as I was instructed.

The officer asked for my license and registration. I told him that I keep my registration under the passenger seat because my glove compartment is full of other stuff. After I told him this information, I asked if it would be okay to reach under the seat to get it. He said, "Yes."

I got the documentation (slowly), along with my license, and handed it to the officer. He looked it over and told me why he had pulled me over. I honestly didn't know it was illegal to flash my lights.

He asked me where I had been and where I was going. I answered. I told him I had come from the grocery store, and I was going to a fast food restaurant before heading home. He nodded his head and made a remark about the inventory of groceries he saw my backseat with the dog.

We had a civil conversation. He took my documents back to the car to check me and my tag out. He came back to the car, handed me my paperwork, gave a slight scolding, and informed me he was going to let me off with a warning. I was grateful, and I thanked the officer for his generosity.

Every time I have been pulled over by the police, I exercise my best behavior. I do as instructed, and whether I get a ticket or not, we both walk away at the end of the day as we began it — alive.

It's a dangerous job. They're constantly putting their life on the line. Many get killed and injured all the time. Every time they put on the uniform their nerves are on edge. The pay is pathetic, and it's practically a thankless job.

When you deal with the police, you need to understand this. I don't think any of them get up in the morning with an idea to go out and kill somebody. I have watched many online live feeds from these protests. This is where you see and hear things the media will not share with you.

I have watched these protesters get inches from officers' faces and hurl profanity and insults at them nonstop. Some do it with bullhorns at full volume.

From a spiritual standpoint, that does affect them. Words are powerful.

In the eighteenth chapter of the book of Proverbs God tells us, "Death and life are in the power of the tongue, and those who love it will eat its fruit."

They throw items, bricks, frozen water bottles, fireworks, and all sorts of things. The police stand there like unmovable statues and take it. I would like to think I could handle it. I have a feeling I would snap and just be all up in somebody's face with a few choice words. That's why I am not on the police force.

Ethan Graham

Do All Lights Matter?

Yes. God said they do, and His authority on the subject is greater than the combination of every voice on earth in unison. He should know. He made us in His image, so why complain about the color wrapping paper he used?

Although, you wouldn't know all lives matter to look at the scene unfolding in this country. Well, to be honest, most countries around the world.

It is easy to think that the world has gone insane. People are fighting over ideologies, political parties, physical differences, religious differences, money, possessions, thoughts, and about anything else you can think of. Nothing is off limits anymore.

Make no mistake, **WE ARE AT WAR!** The propaganda machine is pushing the narrative of war every hour on the hour. They attempt to divide us in any way they can, and then they instruct us why we need to go to war with each other.

The wars people fight amongst each other are irrelevant to the powers that be. They just want the war. It appears we are being attacked by Marxist terrorists with the goal of the total destruction of modern civilization ,and the transfer of all power to their elite overlords. A worldwide coup.

They push a war about race. The

war of the sexes. The war of political parties. The war of agendas. The war of conspiracies. The war of class. The war money. The war of land. War of food. War of seeds and resources. The war of religion. Wars abroad and wars at home.

There is now a war over thought and expression for specific groups only, f course. They all play into the two big wars:

- The war of fear.
- The war against God.

Did you know, that during the weekend of June 5-6, 2020, the number one hashtag trending on social media was #AttackAndDethroneGod? Yes, it was.

Save America: Only Christians Can Do It

Changing the Laws

The world, mostly the Western world, is under attack. As an American, I will concentrate on the U.S. Make no mistake, my rant and observations apply to most other countries out there. We are all at war with the same enemy.

The United States has been pushed, and prodded, to legislate sin as quickly as possible. Why? Because it makes sin more palatable. It smooths out the rough edges, and over time, presents itself as normal.

Oh, it's just this or that, they say. Everybody does it, so there's nothing wrong with it. Then twenty years later, the next generation has been raised to accept and believe a *new normal*.

Over the last decade, there has been a mad rush to change laws in a massive, and socially altering way. My first thought of an example is, believe it or not, gaining ground.

Most people are unaware of the fact that there are groups and organizations that advocate the legalization of pedophilia and child pornography. Check out the new *H.R. 5 Equality Act* coming up before the Congress in the Spring/Summer of 2021.

This thing is loaded with nasty and

unbelievable things. A lot of things that take away parent's rights and authority. Some claim the language could open a back door to legal pedophilia. Could that be true?

There are ongoing movements in many countries around the world to lower the age of consent to that of twelve. The endgame appears to be to abolish the age of consent completely.

Many reading this may say, *That will never happen*. Look at everything that has been legalized up to this date. Many things people thought would never happen in a million years, has indeed happened. Many activities that were once illegal are now legal.

The newest movement being pushed by the media is to defund the police and redirect those funds to other community organizations. Well, as the popular saying goes: *Past proves present*. When I look to the past, I see many reallocated and congressional funds going to pet projects that enrich and empower the elite. We all know where that defunded police money will go.

If you truly defund the police, I would think many officers would have to quit their jobs because they cannot continue to support themselves and their families. I would also assume that the number of police personnel left to service an area would be so limited that they would lose the battle of maintaining law and order completely.

If there are no police, crime can run amok. Anarchy will rise uncontrolled. Then what? Here's a theory to toss out there. When you see a country fall into anarchy, and crime runs unchecked and out of control while gangs rule the streets, what usually happens? The United Nations may send troops.

True, it is against the charter of the United Nations to have a standing army. My observations see their standing army as their *peacekeeping troops*. They sure appear to look and operate like an army. I saw a protester on TV last summer waving a huge, crisp, clean UN flag. Why? A one world movement? I mean, where does one come across a UN flag in Seattle?

There is indeed a one world movement, and have no doubt, the powers that be would love to take control of the United States. If they do that, your freedom is gone. Your civil rights are gone. The Constitution is gone. What will you be left with?

Foreign troops on American soil? That is what I was told. The first I heard of it was around 2009. I was informed by a guy, who had recently left the service, that Iraqi troops were training on the

Mississippi and Russian troops were in the Ozarks. I argued about the legality of foreign troops on American soil. He just shook his head. Was he lying? I don't know.

That was the first time I heard about foreign troops on American soil, but it was not the last. Many foreign service personnel go through special training on our bases. Why? It think of the shooting on the naval base in Pensacola.

Three American millinery officers murdered, and thirteen other injured, on a Naval base in Pensacola. Who did it? Foreigners from the Saudi Arabian Air Force. Now there is a law suit filled against Saudi Arabia by the families. Why are foreign military training inside the U.S. for anything? Anything?

I have also heard of Chinese troops on the southern Mexican border. Again, are these rumors, conspiracy or truth?

I've also heard that they are waiting to be activated. If this is true, and they are activated and come on American soil, is it not possible that they could be joined by invading troops from other countries? How about Jihadists within the country already established? Anarchists within our own borders? Is this true? Could it happen?

The US military is scattered thick abroad with few left on home soil. The new administration wants to deploy a massive number of troops abroad.

What if there were no police because they were defunded and done away with? What defenses are left? What if they take away our Second Amendment to own and bear arms? The right to take those arms and rise up against an unlawful government is gone? That's what all the fuss over the Second Amendment is really about. Our rights to rise up and overthrow them.

I digress. Back to a possible invasion. No matter what the circumstances, most Americans would have a very difficult time following an order to kill fellow Americans. I don't think that would be the case for members of foreign troops or anti-American militant groups.

If this is indeed the truth, we have been infiltrated with the intent of total destruction and annihilation of our country and its inhabitants. Why and by whom?

Who Is the Enemy?

Who Is the Enemy? The narrative being push is trying to indoctrinate me to believe that it's anyone that looks or thinks differently than myself. They keep repeating the same propaganda over and over hoping that it will take root and come to fruition. It seems to me they want as many wars as possible here at home.

Another war we are fighting is the war of disinformation and propaganda. This war does its best to work people into a frenzy and sell fear. This accomplishes two things. First, it gets people to override their normal logic and emotions so they will behave differently. As a person thinks, so are they.

This type of mental abuse, and manipulation, makes people easier to control and push in one particular direction. A bonus for these power hungry people is that it makes them more money.

It's always about following the money, isn't it? For example, in 2020 everybody stayed glued to the media of their choice. Consuming as much information on current events as possible because they were afraid of the situation at hand, or because they agree with the anarchy. Those media outlets will make more money as a result. The higher the viewer count, the more money can be charge per ad. That's why they continually sell fear.

That fear will keep you glued to the media outlets while they raise their ratings,, and thus, increasing their bottom line.

Media, in my opinion, have become the pushers of propaganda. Increasingly, propaganda is glorified by these pushers, and they take their orders from their puppet masters; the elite we will call them. Most of these people hide in the darkest corners where they take their instruction from ancient spirits.

Ancient spirits? I know some you are thinking, *Are you crazy? You just lost me on this one.* I understand, but hear me out. Who are these ancient spirits I'm speaking about? The propaganda pushes the narrative they are aliens, and they are returning to earth on the mother ship soon.

The truth is they are not little green men from Mars. They are not Reptilian's, nor are they Gray's. They are the fallen angels, powers, principalities, and demons talked about in the Bible. Their last infiltration was almost cataclysmic to the human race.

However, God stepped in and save the humananity with a massive worldwide flood. To some people, this may seem like a sci-fi fantasy thriller, but I assure you it is very real. If you're a Christian, you know they are real.

These dark entities are being invited back into our world through the use of quantum computers (which basically tap into parallel universes and make computations). That statement alone is bizarre enough to freak most people out, but it is much deeper than that.

In a more simplistic explanation, I view quantum computers as a four-dimensional spiritual medium. By all appearances, it seems some are using quantum computers, along with particle colliders, to rip the veil that separates our world from theirs. These fallen, dark spirits were put there for a reason.

A few years back, there was a man doing a presentation for computer engineers. He called them dark entities, "...super intelligent aliens..." at a conference in Vancouver.

The last slide of his presentation during that conference had the following quote: *...mission is to be the first to human-level AI. We are hiring demonologist software engineers. Join us.*

Demonologist software engineers? Did I read that right? Yes, I did. I paused the video to make sure (the link is in the Bibliography). Perhaps you may want to rethink the validity of my statement about ancient spirits.

AI, or artificial intelligence, is very dangerous ground. In my opinion, it is probably the most forbidden piece of fruit on the Tree of Knowledge. The entire point of the Tree of Knowledge was that Adam and Eve wanted to be like God.

Increasingly, many people want to be God. They want to decide what is right and what is wrong. They want to make the rules and laws that govern the world in which we live. There are people messing with the human genome and altering DNA of humans and animals.

They genetically modify the food we eat, build machines in an attempt to manipulate the weather, use insects for bio warfare, dump chemicals in the water and the air, bombard us with electromagnetic fields and short microwaves.

They mentally abuse people with their tactics and propaganda, and drain you of your finances in multiple ways. They are breaking up the family unit and destroying lives in the process. They attempt to control the rest of us through fear and other evil activities.

Recently, it seems to me they are trying to control world economies with a virus. A germ. It's simple high school biology. A germ is a bacteria, virus, protozoa, or fungi. When have you ever seen the world forced to shut down for a germ? It all seems to be so well orchestrated and planned.

Perhaps my perspective on the situation is wrong, but I know what I see and hear. I would have never believed the world could shut down that fast.

They pushed a new narrative that this virus was the mother of all plagues, and we must hide to save ourselves. We must remain indoors and away from each other.

This stops us from talking and communicating through private means. It trains you to live, and rely, on a digital system void of human interaction and touch.

Divide and conquer. I heard a preacher recently say that forced isolation, when you are not ill or a danger to others, is not the definition of quarantine. It is one of control.

I read an article that it also helps to lower our immune system function. The longer the isolation, the more susceptible you're going to be to basic germs when you get back out into the real world.

Many want us to wear a mask at all times. Most doctors claim that will only make the air we breathe unhealthy. Using a mask long term can cause carbon dioxide to build up in our lungs and lower the oxygen count in our blood.

Now two masks. No three masks... two masks again...then back to three. Wear it for a month to flatten the curve... another month...one more...no, until the end of the year...wait, end of 2021.

They demand we douse our hands with alcohol-based products, that many doctors say, will lower our immune system. Last year there was recall of nine different alcohol-based sanitizers due to some serious issues. I read it, although, I never heard in through main media outlets.

If this amazing germ is so courageous, allow to pose a few questions:

- Why does it mostly affect Western countries?

- Why do heavily populated countries like China and India appear to fare better?

- Why do crowded, impoverished countries fare better?

- Why didn't the rioters of 2020 drop dead all over the streets from all the close contact and lack of masks?

The social media police, on several platforms, will knock you off line if you mention taking vitamin C or getting plenty of sunshine. You cannot mention anything other than what the accepted guidelines state. There are claims being promoted by various national and international organizations that seem to ignore basic science. Why aren't they promoting fresh air and sunshine?

If breaking down your physical and mental health isn't enough, they have included your finances. They get to decide what business is and is not essential. All legal businesses are essential in my opinion. They are essential to the people who own them and the people who work for them. They are essential to the families who rely on those incomes and services.

This has forced many businesses to close. Guess what! As these small businesses went under, they were purchase for pennies on the dollar, by the huge corporate conglomerates. Wow!

People are kicked to the curb. I have seen my own parents denied basic ongoing health care because doctor offices were shut down.

Americans have been arrested for opening their businesses to the public, and for social distancing and hygiene violations. However, it is okay for thousands to conjugate on the streets, ignore all social distancing rules, riot and loot. Oh, you can see the logic in that, can't you?

It is a full assault. You cannot earn a living, socialize, get basic services due to the pandemic, but you can riot, loot, and steel property form government and the private sector to build autonomous zones.

The virus tests have been proven inaccurate. The case numbers are proven incorrect, yet nothing is enforced for protesters. I guess they have super immunity.

So why a vaccination for a basic germ? Why force people? Why threaten them? Why strip away rights and privileges if you do not get one.

Which one is *the one*? The vaccination that comes in one shot or two? From drug company A, B, C, D or E? Is it the shot that stays stable at room temperature or the one that needs to be kept in the deep freeze?

It was a one-shot deal. Now they say you will need it every year. Some say every two months. The new narrative claims that the mirracle vaccination will not allow you to stop wearing a mask. You need it for protection.

Why are there some many different vaccines for one virus? How is a vaccine created for a virus that has no isolates? Why was the flu so low in 2020? Why did the UK have not one single reported case of the flu in 2020?

At the height of the panic stressing hospitals to the max, they were proven to be empty time and time again by people walking through them with video cameras. My cousin works a hospital. She said they had twenty-three people admitted. This was during big *Sky is Falling* time in 2020.

The internet was loaded with people showing this truth. It was also loaded with doctors and nurses dancing. Where did they find the energy and time while triaging patients in the parking because they were filled to capacity? When Trump sent he Navy ships, Mercy and Comfort for their use...why did they stay practically empty of these ill patients?

My favorite online video was a woman in Dublin, Ireland who walked through a empty place; not one person was there. I guess the medical team was at the pub having a pint.

The Irish TV media said the facility was overflowing. I know because this woman told you all about it. She named the shows and the reporters. She even quoted a few. This woman kept, walking through the place saying, "There's nobody bloody here! The whole thing is a lie. There's nobody bloody here!"

After that, every time I saw a online video of someone filming an empty hospital, I would always laugh and say, "There's nobody bloody here!" I don't know who that woman is, but I love her. Sadly, her video was removed. I hope she reposted somewhere.

This pandemic is, in my opinion, an excuse for everything. They are trying to shutdown life through this so-called pandemic. I only see three pandemics going on currently:

- Fear
- Terrorism
- Propaganda

I return to the question at the beginning of this chapter. Who is the enemy? If you say the socialist puppet masters controlling the world, I would give you a passing grade.

However, the correct answer is the dark entities, demons, and spirits the puppet masters, and their minions, have given themselves to. The ones they are communicating with. The ones whose bidding they do here on earth. The ones they have appeared to yield themselves to an exchange for money, power, and the chance to be a god. They have sold their fellow humans out for thirty pieces of silver.

These are the ones they are pledging their allegiance to when they take a knee. There are serious, dark powers behind all this mess. Do not kneel to it. Do not submit to it. Better to die standing free than live than be enslaved to demonic beings.

There is one important fact you

should remember in your life. Jesus told us in the book of John chapter ten, "The thief does not come except to steal, and to kill, and to destroy. I have come that they may have life, and that they may have it more abundantly." The thief, of course, is Satan.

Therefore, always remember that when you are attacked, mistreated, assaulted, lied about, abused and any other horrible thing that can happen to you at the hands of other human beings. You must remember who has hurt you.

Was it the human that hurt you? Yes. Remember to delve deeper. Because at the root...is the devil.

He is the one hiding behind the mask. Whatever human has hurt you, they allowed the devil to use their body, their words, and their actions to hurt you.

The devil comes to kill, to steal, and to destroy. Those are the devil's fingerprints. Therefore, you know who to blame in the end for all the bad things that happened to you at the hands of others, and sometimes, he uses you against your own self.

Let's take a look at what is happening to Americans right now as an example. The country with more freedoms than any other on earth is being killed. The peace and love of the citizens of this country are being stolen, and the heart of the country is being destroyed. The enemy is not the person you think it is. It is the devil operating through that person, organization, or system.

Was This Day Foretold?

The first official president of the United States, George Washington, may have been used to warn us, and to offer hope. It seems that General George Washington was given a vision from God during Valley Forge. This is what Anthony Sherman, a soldier who served with him at Valley Forge, told a reporter named Charles Wesley Alexander (who frequently wrote under the pseudonym of Wesley Bradshaw).

Some historians have accused Mr. Alexander of making a few embellishments to make his interview appear more exclusive. Maybe he did.

Mr. Sherman (age 90 at the time) reportedly sat in Independence Hall with Mr. Alexander and shared his first account experience of hearing Gen.ral George Washington share his vision experience with others at Valley Forge.

There were murmurings of this vision circulating before it was printed for the general public. The details Mr. Sherman shared were printed in a Mormon periodical in 1856.

It then appeared in *The Philadelphia Inquirer* in 1861. The first general publication was in *The Tribune News* in 1859. It was later reprinted by The

Tribune News in 1880 by requests from readers.

It has been reprinted in multiple publications since. As it is now public domain, it is widely available online. Below is the article printed in *The Tribune News* from the December issue in 1880.

SECOND PRINT: 1880
THE NATIONAL TRIBUNE
VOLUME 4, NUMBER 12 – DECEMBER 1880
PUBLISHED BY THE NATIONAL TRIBUNE COMPANY IN WASHINGTON DC

WASHINGTON'S VISION

"The last time I ever saw Anthony Sherman was on the Fourth of July, 1859, in Independence Square. He was then ninety-nine years old, and becoming very feeble; but, those so old, his dimming eyes rekindled as he gazed upon Independence Hall, which he had come to gaze upon once more before he was gathered home.

"Let us go to the Hall," he said. "I want to tell you an incident of Washington's life — one which no one alive knows of except myself, and if you look live you will before long see it verified. Mark the prediction, you will see it verified. * * * From the opening of the Revolution We Experienced All Phases of Fortune — Now Good and Now Ill, Onetime Victorious in Another Concord. The Darkest. We Had, I Think, Was When Washington, after Several Reverses, Retreated to Valley Forge, Where He Resolved to Pass the Winter of seventeen seventy-seven. Ah! I have often seen the cheers coursing down our dear old commander's careworn cheeks as he would be conversing with a confidential officer about the condition of his poor soldiers. You have doubtless heard the story of Washington going to the thicket to pray. Well, it was not only true, but he used to often to pray in secret for aid and comfort from God, the interposition of whose Divine Province brought us safely through those dark days of tribulation."

"One day, I remember it well, the chili wins whispered through the leafless trees, though the sky was cloudless and the sun shone brightly; he remained in his quarters nearly all the afternoon alone. When he came out, I noticed his face was a shape paler than usual, and there seem to be something on his mind of more than ordinary importance. Returning just after dusk, he dispatched an orderly to the quarters of the officer I mentioned, who was presently in attendance. After a preliminary conversation, which lasted about half an hour, Washington, gazing upon his companions with a strange look of dignity which he alone could command, said to the latter: 'I do not know whether it is owing to the anxiety of my mind, or what, but this afternoon as I was sitting at the very table engaged in preparing a dispatch, something in the apartment seem to disturb me. Looking up, I beheld standing opposite to me a singularly beautiful female. So astonished was I, for I had given strict orders not to be disturbed, that it was some moments before I found language to inquire the cause of her presence. A second, a third, and even a fourth time did I repeat my question, but received no answer from my mysterious visitor is set a slight raising of the eyes. By this time, I felt strange sensations spreading through me. I would have risen but the riveted gaze of the being before me rendered volition impossible. I essayed once more to address her, but my tongue had become powerless. Even thought, itself suddenly became paralyzed. A new influence, mysterious, potent, irresistible, took possession of me. All I could do was to gaze steadily, vacantly, at my unknown visitant. Gradually the surrounding atmosphere seemed as though becoming filled with sensations and grew luminous. Everything about me seemed to rarify, the mysterious visitor herself becoming more-airy, and yet even more distant to my site than before. I now began to feel as one dying or rather to experience the sensations which I have some, times imagine a company dissolution. I did not think, I did not reason, I did not move; all were alike impossible. I was only conscious of gazing fixedly, vacantly, at my companion.'

'Presently I heard a voice saying, "Son of the Republic, look and learn," while at the same time I visitor extended her arm East Woodley. I now be held a heavy white vapor at some distance rising fold upon fold. This gradually dissipated, and I looked upon the strange scene.

Before me lay spread out and one vast plain all the countries of the world — Europe, Asia, Africa, and America. I saw a rolling and tossing between Europe and America the billows of the Atlantic, and between Asia and America lay the Pacific. "Son of the Republic," said the same mysterious voices before, "look and learn." At that moment I beheld the dark, shadowy being like an angel standing, or, rather, floating, in mid-air between Europe and America. Dripping water out of the ocean in the hollow of each hand, he sprinkled some upon America with his right hand, while with his left hand he cast some upon Europe. Immediately a dark cloud raised from each of these countries and joined in mid-ocean. For a while it remains stationary, and then move slowly westward, until it enveloped America in its murky folds. Sharp flashes of lightning gleaned through it as intervals, and I heard the smothered groans and cries of the American people. A second time the angel dipped water from the ocean and sprinkled it out as before. The dark cloud was then drawn back to the ocean, in whose having waves it sank from view.'

'A third, I heard the mysterious voice saying: "Son of the Republic, look and learn." I cast my eyes upon America in beheld villages and towns and cities bringing up one after another, until the whole land from the Atlantic to the Pacific was dotted with them. Again, I heard the mysterious voice say: "Son of the Republic, the end of the country, look and learn." At this the dark shadowy angel turned his face southward, and from Africa I saw and ill-omened spirit approach our land. It flitted slowly and heavily over town and city of the latter; the inhabitants presently set themselves in battle array against each other. As I continue looking, I saw a bright angel, on whose brow rested a crown of light, on which was traced *UNION*, bearing the American flag, which was placed between the divided nation, and said: "Remember, your brethren." Instantly the inhabitants, casting from their weapons, became friends once more and united around the national standard.'

'And again, I heard the mysterious voice saying: "Son of the Republic, the end of the century, look and learn." At this the dark shadowy angel placed a trumpet to his mouth and blew three distinct blasts, and taking water from the ocean he sprinkled it upon Europe, Asia, and Africa. Then my eyes beheld a fearful scene. From each of these countries arose thick black clouds that were soon joined into one. And throughout this masa there gleamed a dark red light, by which I saw the hordes of armed men, who, moving with the cloud, march by land and sailed by sea to America, which country was enveloped in the volume of the cloud. And I distinctly saw these fast armies devastate the whole country and burn the villages, towns, and cities that I beheld springing up. As my tears listened to the thundering of Canon, clashing of swords, and shouts and cries of millions in mortal combat, I again heard the mysterious voice saying: "Son of the Republic, look and learn."

'When the voice had ceased the dark shadowy angel places trumpet once more to his mouth and blew a long, powerful blasts. Instantly alight, as if of a thousand suns, shone down from above me, and pierced and broke into fragments the dark cloud which enveloped America. At the same moment I saw the Angel upon whose head still shown the word *UNION*, and who bore our national flag in one hand and a sword in the other, to send from Heaven attended by legions of bright spirits. These immediately joined the inhabitants of America who, I perceived, were well-nigh overcome, but who, immediately taking courage again, closed up their broken ranks and renewed the battle. Again, amid the fearful noise of the conflict, I heard the mysterious voice saying: "Son of the Republic, look and learn." As the voice ceased, the shadowy angel for the last time dipped water from the ocean and sprinkled it upon America. Instantly the dark cloud rolled back, together with the armies it had brought, leaving the inhabitants of the land victorious. Then, once more, I beheld villages, towns, and cities bringing up where there had been before, while the bright angel, planting the standard he had brought in the midst of them, cried in a loud voice: "While the stars remain in the heavens send down do upon the earth, so long shall the Republic last." And taking from his brow the crown, on which blazoned the word *UNION*, he placed it upon the standard, while the people, kneeling down, said, "Amen." '

'The scene instantly began to fade and dissolve, and I at last saw nothing but the rising, curling vapor I had at first beheld. This also disappearing, I fell myself once more gazing on my mysterious visitor, who, in the same voice I heard before said: "Son of the Republic, what ye have seen is thus interpreted: Three perils will come upon the Republic. The most fearful is third, which the whole world united shall never be able to prevail against her. Let every child of the Republic learn to live for his God, his land, and the Union." With these words the vision vanished, and I started from my seat and felt that I had seen a vision where and had been shown me the birth, progress, and destiny of the United States. In union she will have her strength, in disunion her destruction.'

"Such, my friends," continued the venerable narrator, "were the words I heard from Washington's own lips, and America will do well to profit by then."

— Wesley Braushaw

What Does It All Mean?

Everybody is in agreement of the interpretation the first two perils.

The first peril describes an angel sprinkling water from the Atlantic Ocean, with its right hand on America with the left hand on Europe.

A dark cloud arose from each continent, joined in the middle of the ocean, and slowly drifted over America.

The groans of the American people were heard until the cloud withdrew and disappeared.

Afterward we see towns come into being all over the United States from the East Coast to the Pacific Coast. Most people unanimously agree that this is the Revolutionary War that was currently in progress at the time of vision.

England came across the sea to fight a war on American shores. After independence was won, America began to grow and expand Westward towards the Pacific Ocean.

The second peril shows an angel looking towards Africa. Washington saw an ill-omened spirit approach the United States. It was a slow and heavy spirit that hovered over the land.

The people then prepared their selves for battle against each other.

Another angel appeared with the word *UNION* on his four head and it was holding the American Standard, or flag.

That angel place the divided flag between the nation itself and told people to remember that they were brothers. The vision shows Americans discarding their weapons and becoming united once more around the American Standard. Again, most people agree on this interpretation being the Civil War.

Human traffickers were losing their trade in England and Europe, and started trafficking people over from Africa to be enslaved in the Caribbean and in North America.

There were many disagreements between the northern and southern states. When the South seceded from the Union, Abraham Lincoln was determined not to let them go. He had many reasons for this.

However, after much loss, and complaining from the northern states that he should just let the South go on its own, his cause found renewed strength and investment from the abolitionists.

The country was saved, and Americans once again became United. The war started over the southern state's succession from the union for many reasons; especially taxation. However, the war of secession soon transformed into a war about the abolishment of slavery in America.

The third peril is open for interpretation. An angel blows three distinct blast on a trumpet. Again, water is taken from the ocean and sprinkled upon Europe, Asia, and Africa.

Thick, dark clouds rose from these continents and joined together. There were hordes of armed troops moving by land and sea to the United States.

America was enveloped in this cloud and devastated with war and the towns were burned. The sounds of a horrible battle were audibly heard, and the Angel once again blew another blast on the trumpet.

Washington saw a light like a thousand suns break through the dark cloud covering America. The cloud was broken into fragments, as the angel with the American Standard, descended.

Americans closed in their ranks. The angel once again sprinkled ocean water across America, the cloud and armies reseed, and America is victorious. The angel places the American Standard as the people were kneeling and saying, "Amen."

From today's map, we can see many hostilities against the US and Europe. Some of these hostilities are among Europeans, but most are from the European Arab and North African immigrants who come from anti-American countries.

Asia consist of the People's Republic of China and the Russian Federation. One communist, and the other formally communist. Both have a heavy disdain for the United States. That leaves us with Africa, which is increasingly being taken over by Muslims, many of which, are very anti-American.

America has many enemies around the world who burn the American flag in their streets while chanting death to America. These people joining forces in a war against the United States is not unimaginable.

There are trade wars, proxy wars, cold wars, religious wars, policy wars, and even currency wars; specifically, BRICS in recent years.

If it is indeed true that there are foreign troops on American soil waiting for martial law to be declared to attack us. It is not totally unimaginable that they will send reinforcement troops from their home countries. This would be a devastating battle on American soil.

That would match what Washington saw. Here I will reiterate…

With our own military scattered abroad

If the police are defunded and dismantled

The economy devastated due to shutdowns over a germ

People's immune systems grow weak due to wearing masks

We have been separated from each other due to social distancing

We may be sitting ducks. Perhaps the *new normal* is a set up? Perhaps this is just a precursor.

The last trumpet blast from the Angel depicting the light of a thousand suns, many be interpreted as a nuclear blast. Others see it as the power and mercy of God coming to America's defense and rescue because, we see in the latter part of the vision, the people were on their knees before God.

Therefore, many assume that America turned from her sins, repented and asked for God's help and mercy. The light is God's deliverance. I tend to believe the latter because I cannot imagine a nuclear attack being launched on the United States without the American military reciprocating. If that happens it is game over for the world.

Slavery...Let's Go There

There are two major types of slavery. Slavery from the past and slavery in the present. It takes many forms. Let's tackle slavery from the past.

The first thing that comes to my mind when I hear the word slavery, as an American, is the Civil War. The second thought that comes to my head is my fifth-grade teacher.

Being a student in her class was a

dream come true. It is the only time in my life I actually got the teacher I wanted. On the first day of school, I was so happy to see my name on her door.

We only had two African-American teachers in my school, and she was one of them. She was intelligent, fair and a sharp dresser. I remember having a conversation with her when I was in the fourth grade. That is when I made the decision, I wanted her to be my teacher in fifth grade. I'm very grateful I got in her class.

On a personal note, our history book that year was about the African continent. I remember my first lessons in school about the Civil War were from that book. I seem to recall there were only about four or five white kids in my class.

She made it very clear that there would be no racial discussions in her classroom because none of us, or our parents or grandparents, were alive when the war happened. She said, "The only wars they remembered was World War II, Korea and Vietnam."

She also made it known that many white people had been sold into slavery through a crooked indentured servant program in early America and never gained their freedom back. They work side by side with slaves of color.

She also told us white Europeans were sold as slaves in North Africa over several centuries. She went on to highlight other slave trades throughout history and taught us that, basically, almost every civilization has had their hand at enslaving another group of people at some point in time. I had never heard such a thing.

I remember her pulling out very old history books and teaching things that had been omitted from our classroom book. I encountered this one other time with my tenth grade US History teacher who had old books, periodicals, and original film footage from World War II that showed a different history than the one that was being taught.

My fifth grade teacher had very strong opinions about Abraham Lincoln, and she was not a fan. She basically believed that Lincoln never went to war to free the slaves in the southern states She felt his sole purpose was to preserve the Union, and he used the abolitionists to help him achieve that goal.

She was also very adamant about her disdain for the *Three-Fifths Compromise*. I found this all shocking from an African-American woman. This was not the narrative I had been taught. I also remember other strong statements she made in regards to slavery.

I bring all this up because the issue is still brewing in the twenty-first century. Therefore, in the spirit of my fifth grade teacher, I want to offer a brief snapshot of slavery throughout the world. There are basically three types of slavery: chattel, debt bondage and contractual forced labor.

I think almost all readers of this book are very familiar with the slave trade in the United States. Slaves were not only in the southeast section of the country. They were in the northeast, and there was also a slave trade in the territories out West.

By the time the Civil War rolled around, most of the slaves were in the southeast exclusively. After the *Emancipation Proclamation*, all slaves became free in the United States.

The institution of slavery was never reestablished in the country, but things changed in 1877 when the Democratic Party took control in the southern states. When this happened, African-Americans began to lose everything they achieved during the Reconstruction era.

As time under the power of the Democratic Party continued, the African-American community lost political power and the right to vote. They became second-class citizens in their own country. The majority lived in poverty as farmers and sharecroppers.

I find this fervent call from the current Democratic Party, to tear down all traces of the Confederacy ,ironic considering the involvement of their party transitioning freed African-Americans back into a second-class form of enslavement. It's rather like them trying to destroy their own history so nobody is the wiser.

That being said, let me make it

abundantly clear I am not a Republican. Neither am I a Democrat for that matter. I have voted for both parties, and I have voted for independent and libertarian candidates too. One time I even voted for someone who had no political party affiliation.

I refuse to allow myself to be aligned with any political party and be dictated by it. I want to vote for the best man or woman for the job. However, most times I am forced to vote for the lesser of the two evils.

Let's take a brief look at some of the slavery in human history:

- During the Atlantic Slave trade, many power leaders in the West African were involved in the trade. They captured and sold their own kinsmen, from rival tribes, as slaves to European (American, British, French, and Portuguese) traders that transported them to be sold in various countries.

- The Roman armies made several notations in their records that the Celtic tribes in northwest Europe owned slaves. Saint Patrick himself was captured and enslaved by the Celts. In a letter to the soldiers of Coroticus he is quoted as saying, "...slaves could become a form of internal or trans-border currency."

- The barbaric attacks and enslavement by the Nordic tribes from Scandinavia are quite famous. Europe was terrified of the Vikings. They enslaved some people for their own use, but they usually sold them to the Byzantine or Islamic slave traders.

- The Romanians enslaved many Italians and peoples of Europe.

- The British Isles had voluntary servitude and debt slavery until 1066, and operated slave ships.

- Korea had slavery until 1894.

- India has engaged in slavery throughout its history.

- Tibet has traded slaves and forced boys into monastic slavery.

- Many kingdoms in Africa have practiced several forms of slavery.

- Myanmar currently has had many problems with forced labor.

- Mongols enslaved men, women and children. Some were used and sold within the Mongolia region while others were sold to the Russia's. They also invaded Russia for slaves.

- Slavery was illegal in the Netherlands, but it was legal throughout the Dutch empire.

- Italy sold Slavic, Turks, Georgians, and other people's from the Baltic regions of the Black Sea and the Caucasus. Of course, ancient Rome had slaves

- Ancient Greece had slaves.

- France, Norway and Denmark all abolish slavery in the seventeen hundreds.

- The Barbary Coast slave trade is one of the largest in history, but the seldom talked about. Europeans were sold by North Africans to Muslims. Most historians say it lasted over a thousand years and enslaved millions. There are disagreements among historians about how many people were enslaved. The heart of the trade was heaviest between the sixteenth and eighteenth centuries. The reason for that is because the slave trade on the Barbary Coast in North Africa had existed since antiquity. Therefore, it's hard to calculate due to lack of records. Barbary pirates raided Europe in search of white Christian Europeans to sell on the North African coast to Muslims.

- Egypt had slaves.

- There is a history of Native Americans owning slaves.

- Hawaii had slaves.

- New Zealand had slaves captured as prisoners of war.

- Russia had slaves until the early seventeenth century when Peter the Great came along.

- The Tartar's from Turkey enslaved tens of thousands of Ukrainians.

- The Philippines also practiced slavery with the Muslims.

- Portugal enslaved people including native of Brazil.

- Denmark and Ireland ran slave auction markets for Anglos and Celts in the Barbary slave trade.

- Poland had slavery until the fifteenth century.

- Japan had slavery within its own island boundaries up into the late sixteenth century. Despite this fact, contractual slavery and indentured servant practices prevailed up to the Pacific War.

- Thailand and Burma were victims of slavery.

- There has been slavery in Indonesia.

- Siam had slavery.

- There has been some form of slavery on every continent.

There are more examples, but I'm not going to offer an exhaustive list. I encourage you to do your own research if you are interested.

Quite frankly. We can't possibly list them all. All throughout history countries and tribes have fought with one another and taken each other as prisoners of war and enslaved them.

They are no complete records.

All the ancient empires had slavery: the Byzantines, the Assyrians, Babylonians, the Persians and the list goes on. Throughout history, all continents have been involved. No one escapes the issue of slavery.

I prefer not to dwell on the past sins of slavery that have since been abolished. I can educate myself about it. I can learn from it, but I don't want to live in the past. I would rather concentrate my energy on slavery that exist today.

Now let's talk about slavery in the present. Human trafficking, sex trafficking, work camps and other forms of slavery that still exist in certain parts of the world. Slavery in 2021 A.D.!

How many children are stolen from their families to fight in drug and territorial wars in Africa? How many women are stolen to be used as sex slaves in Africa? I think of those poor Chibok Christian schoolgirls abducted by Muslims in 2014. Some escaped and have told the horrors they experienced.

There are enslaved people in work camps in North Korea, Myanmar and China. In an article from 2015 entitled, *India: The Center of Modern Slavery?* it stated that over 14,000,000 Eastern Indians are victims of some form of modern slavery.

The UN reports that chattel slavery in Islamic North Africa still exist today. Also, debt bondage slavery practices still continue in many countries around the world and religious slavery as well

There are places in India, Pakistan and Nepal were poor families offer up their daughters to the priests, or gods , as temple prostitutes to atone for their sins—or to please a god or goddess.

Adults and children are abducted all over the world and sent to various locations to be enslaved in the sex trade industry. This includes infants. There are places that still practice child brides for grown men.

Many women in the United States are screaming they are oppress. They should turn their efforts to help women who truly need liberation. It is estimated that over 27,000,000 human beings are currently victims of modern-day slavery.

There is another form of modern slavery, and it goes by the names of Socialism and Communism. They enslave the general population to a system that serves the elite. It lords over them through fear, tyranny and corruption.

That is where I see this current move trying to take us. It seems to me the real objective at hand in this country, and around the world, is not racial quality. It is about Socialism and Communism taking over and enslaving the people.

We should learn from history that Communism and Marxism never work. Many leaders within the protester groups explain online they are trained in Marxism.

From an American point of view, I also see this agenda and attempt to remove state rights and teach people to bow to federal authority. When that federal authority is controlled by the liberal/progressive/communist/left that have hijacked the current Democrat party, it spells trouble.

It seems they keep trying to implement their socialist and communist agenda upon this country. This is basically what the People's Republic of China, a communist country, does.

These people are using racial inequality, gender inequality, financial inequality (and any other inequality that will fuel the flames of internal war and conflict with each other) to push their agenda to collapse the country and enslave us all. They divide and then they conquer. We must stand united as Americans or we will surely fall and be enslaved side-by-side.

I have ancestors that were enslaved. In my humble opinion, instead of focusing so much energy and anger at something that happened hundreds or thousands of years ago…why not focus on making real change in slavery that exist today?

The slaves of the past, God rest their souls, are no more on this earth. Their pain and suffering is over. We need to help the slaves of today. No longer can we ignore their cries for help.

This brings me back to the question I asked earlier. Do all lives matter? Yes, they do. We cannot do anything about the lives destroyed by slavery in the past, but we can do something about the lives currently being ripped apart by slavery today. Surely, we can unite over this fact.

Ethan Graham

America Only Has One Way Out

I think everybody's eyes have been wide open to the fact of how quickly it can all be taken away. Perhaps we have got a warning shot over the bow, and if we act, God will have mercy and grant us more time. Precious time to do what I believe He has called this nation to do.

We will have more time to get His Gospel out. We have the money, the manpower and the population to do it. We were leading the charge, but starting in the nineteen sixties, many churches (not all) started becoming silent. This was mainly due to the fact that they were now part of the 501C(3) system that makes them accountable to government and not God's people.

We allowed God to be removed from schools, sporting events, our families, our homes, and we are now to the point where God has little place in the public arena of this country.

We continue to pass laws to legislate sin to ensure that no one can speak up and say what you are doing is wrong. Why? Because it is now legal. If they legislate away our rights, our freedoms, and our speech, then they will have rendered us powerless.

Many are trying to rewrite history books once again by declaring that America is not, nor has ever been, a

Christian nation. That simply is not true. That history is well documented.

Can an ideology save the country? No.

Can a social organization save the country? No.

Can money save the country? No.

Can a political party save the country? No.

Can the President of the United States save the country? No.

However, God can use all, or none of the above to do His will. President Trump was attacked by these people daily. He had people within government sabotaging him, backstabbing him and trying to get him out by any means necessary.

They stalled him work and ignored his authority. There are now military persons—more political in ambition than military—who made it known they would be insubordinate to any orders from the President they did not like. That is mutiny.

How will the President look if he gave an other for the military to move in to Seattle and clear out the self-proclaim *People's Republic of C.H.O.P.*, and high ranking members refuse to give the order to the troops. He would look like a powerless president.

If he he skirted around them and went in, most of the media would have labeled him a rebellious tyrant. All cameras would be on standby for any civilian casualty, and he would have been branded a murderer. He could not win.

Many in media distort facts and others flat out lie. Congress stalls with kangaroo court antics. This served two purposes. First, they got to stall all his efforts and policies. Secondly, they utilized a national media platform to promote their propaganda.

Why are these involved parties doing this? Could it be there is a shadow government with another president's orders they are following? Did we have an elected president being unjustly attacked, with the intent to overthrow, by an unelected president attempting a coup?

Irregardless if you voted for Trump or not, no U.S. President has ever been rebelled against in such a manner. It is a terrifying position in which he found himself, yet he took it. With all his wealth, he could bailed and lived a great life of luxury.

Why did he stay and fight? Could it be that he isn't as horrible as the media/celebrity narrative claimed he was? Why live with that pressure when he had the money and power to escape? Could he really be a good guy trying to help save this country from something very dark and evil. Even is that is the case, he cannot do it. He is a mere man.

Do you think Biden will help? Well, with over fifty executive orders... and growing...it does not look good. Bombing s have started abroad, prices are soaring, constitutional rights are fleeing, and a 1.9 trillion dollar bailout for their special interests and friends.

Friends like DC, New York and California get bailout money. Let's look at some other friends. There is $1.5 million for a bridge to connect Canada and the US. Do we need another bridge?

$50 million to groups who help with abortions

$200 million for the The Institute of

Museum and Library Services

Over $800 million to community groups.

Education get $128 billion

Higher education gets only $39 billion

$15 billion for airlines

$86 billion for pension bailouts

$75 billion for more vaccines

Over $250 million for the National Endowment of the Arts

FEMA gets $50 billion

Amtrack gets $1.5 billion

Most estimations conclude over $1 trillion in pocket-stuffing pork

This is the 2021 Stimulus Bill that has passed the House. Wait! You do get up to $1400. Well, maybe. They are talking about lowering that amount. This seems to be what a Biden Administration has to offer. I'm sure there is a little something for the CCP and the Ukraine from 'ol Uncle Joe.

This country needs to be saved from the calamity coming. The world needs to be saved from the same fate. There is only one way to save this country, and it has to be done by Christians. Not black Christians. Not white Christians. Not Asian Christians. Not Native American Christians. No, the Body of Christ must be united.

For too long, many members of the Body of Christ have tried to separate and go out on their own. The Body needs all of its members to function properly. The Body does not function without the brain and the head telling it what to do. Christ is the head, and His Body must be united in this country once again.

In the last several decades, the

American church has looked very stupid moving around dismembered without a head. Corrupt churches have been indoctrinated by the government and has presented itself to the nation as a sheep when it's really a wolf.

No wonder people don't take these Christians seriously. These fake churches have preached a false Christ. They operate in segregation, confusion, and no headship. They have no power. It looks weak and no better than the world around. That's why many in these churches leave. They complain they have done all that was asked of them, but nothing changed. There was no promised fruit.

God has called Christians to be His kings and priests. He has called us to serve Him, and to proclaim His Salvation to the world. He has called us to walk in unity as His Body, to display His love, and His power.

Take a look around you. The country is going to hell in a hand basket. They are rioting in the streets, families are being torn apart, kids are growing up without a father, sexual morality is rampant — so much so that they are teaching it to kindergartners!

Lies and deception rule the day. People are hungry for love and acceptance. They want to belong. Sadly, many are willing to join some dark forces and hateful groups to find that sense of belonging, acceptance and love of others; even if it is lie. Groups led by sorcery and deception.

Many of the, so-called churches, look just like the world. They are wolves. What big teeth grandma has.

Their congregates use profanity, engage in all types of sexual immorality, lie, cheat, steal, and look just like their worldly counterparts. The Body of Christ is dwindling because we are losing Christ in our own lives, so why would anybody want to live like we do? What is it about our lives make people hunger for Christ and His Salvation?

If this country has a chance to survive this and win, it is Christians that have to step up and do what they were called to do. They must be who they were made in Christ to be. It must be done now! We must do it united as one Body with Christ as the head.

Time is up. This is what we must do:

"When I shut up heaven and there is no rain, or command the locusts to devour the land, or send pestilence among My people, if My people who are called by My name will humble themselves, and pray and seek My face, and turn from their wicked ways, then I will hear from heaven, and will forgive their sin and heal their land. Now My eyes will be open and My ears attentive to prayer *made* in this place." II Chronicles 7:13-15

#1

We must humble ourselves before the Lord. This means we have to check our American pride, and any other pride, at the door. We all know Americans are a very proud people.

We are proud of our house, our car, our children, our accomplishments, our careers, our looks, what section of the country were from, our ethnic background, our sex...we tend to be prideful about almost anything.

#2

We, as Christians, have to cry out to God. We must repent before God. We have to ask for forgiveness for our own shortcomings and the sins in our own lives.

We must ask God to forgive us for not being a watchman on the wall, and allowing the enemy to come into this country.

The body of Satan has been bringing in evil spirits, demons, and fallen angels into this country to cause chaos, fear, destruction, and turn people from God and His Salvation. The Body of Christ has failed the Lord in so many areas. We must ask for forgiveness.

#3

We have to turn our backs on the world system and all its trappings. We can't watch a movie or series, and fast-forward through the bad parts and think it's okay. We gotta stop singing curses upon ourselves with worldly music.

Honestly, I had to repent from this

a couple years ago. I had to really stop and listen to the lyrics of some of the songs I was singing.

I'll give you one example. Growing up, I was a huge Michael Jackson fan. I saw a preacher on the Internet a few years ago who tore his music apart, along with others in the pop and the hip-hop industry.

The Michael Jackson stuff really made me stop and think. I remember when I was young, I didn't like the song *Thriller* because it gave me the creeps. However, when I saw the video, I adjusted my way of thinking about the song. I rarely played the song, but I loved watching the video.

This preacher forced me to go over the lyrics. This was easy because I still remember them. I was in shock at the overall message, or meaning, of those lyrics. It wasn't hidden at all. They were in plain view. I understand being deceived as a child, but I've been an adult for quite some time and I never picked up on it. That's how blind I was to it.

When I was a child, I often heard adults in church tell me that popular music was the devil's music, but they never explained why. This preacher, I saw on the Internet, explained why.

I firmly believe, that if an adult would have taken the time to explain to me *why* the lyrics were bad, I would have had no choice but to concur. Instead, I ignored their nay saying and continued to sing many songs, I now understand, were mostly curses upon myself.

I look back, and I can honestly tell you that I see the manifestation of many of those curses. I invite you to go and take a hard look at the lyrics of some of the songs you have been singing; some thousands of times.

I heard a gentleman that worked in the music industry, before he was saved, say that the industry is fully aware of what they are doing. They know they can never get Christians to curse themselves, but they can get them to do it through music. I regret to say I stand guilty as charged. I thank God, through Jesus Christ, I was able to repent and be saved from those curses.

#4

We have been piling up a lot of debris that has blocked our open path of communication with God. I dare say, it is also blocked many of His blessings.

After we humble ourselves, seek God, pray to God, and turned from our evil ways that we have adopted from this world then...THEN...He gives us His

Word that He will hear us. His ears will be attentive to our prayers again. His eyes will be open to our trouble. He will forgive us, and <u>He will heal our land</u>.

In conclusion, God is love. God is just. God is forgiving. God did not abandon us. He did not abandon our country. We abandoned Him.

We let our guard down. We left the gate open. We allowed the enemies to charge in and bring this evil destruction upon our country. It is not the world's fault because they are part of the world system. They don't know any better because they live in darkness.

We, Christians, are the ones to whom the light has been given. Christians are the ones to whom salvation has come. Christians are the ones who have been charged by God to be His kings and priests, and to take His salvation to aworld that lives in darkness.

Christians are to blame for the current situation. Not just in America, but around the world. We have become seekers of pleasure, prideful, and we have abandoned our post and have abandoned our duties.

Therefore, there is only one way out of the chaotic, evil darkness which this country has been enveloped by the powers and principalities of the devil. God's people have to humble themselves before God, seek Him, repent before Him, and turn our backs on evil.

Yes, only God can save us from this mess, but He calls us to action. He demands we repent, humble ourselves and pray. We are to blame for this. We have to call out to Him to fix it. Now, it may be time for the end, but I do not this k it is. I think we will be given one more chance to reach the world with His Salvation.

Repent.

Humble ourselves.

Pray.

This is the only way to clear and re-open that pathway to God, so He can forgive us and once again have that unobstructed, direct line to heal our land and bless us.

And when they had come to the multitude, a man came to Him, kneeling down to Him and saying, "Lord, have mercy on my son, for he is an epileptic and suffers severely; for he often falls into the fire and often into the water. So I brought him to Your disciples, but they could not cure him." Then Jesus answered and said, "Oh faithless and perverse generation, how long shall I be with you? How long shall I bear with you? Bring him here to Me." 18 And Jesus rebuked the demon, and it came out of him; and the child was cured from that very hour. Then the disciples came to Jesus privately and said,

"Why could we not cast it out?" So Jesus said to them, "Because of your [e]unbelief; for assuredly, I say to you, if you have faith as a mustard seed, you will say to this mountain, 'Move from here to there,' and it will move; and nothing will be impossible for you. However, this kind does not go out except by prayer and fasting."   Matthew 14:19-21

I also think we need to fast because many of the powers and principalities over this country are incredibly strong, and they have held their territory for a long time. I don't think they will let it go without a fight.

I call my brothers and sisters in Christ to fast continuously. Every week fast from something. You can fast from a particular food or drink, television, recreational Internet use, an activity you enjoy, and so on. Pick one thing every week to fast from, and dedicate that fast to the Lord.

Fasting, when combined with prayer, will annihilate these powers and principalities holding our country prisoner.

We must unite as one Body with Christ as our head. We must humble ourselves, seek God, and turn from our sins as His united Body. We must call on God to forgive us and heal our land. We must ask Him to give us another opportunity to be a light in a world of darkness, so those who are lost may find their way to Him and His Salvation.

We must stand in the gap because no one else can do it. It is time to rise up Christians. Rise up and be the priests and kings you are called, and anointed, to be. Put on the full armor of God, in Jesus' Name, and rise up!

"O you afflicted one, tossed with tempest, and not comforted, Behold, I will lay your stones with colorful gems, and lay your foundations with sapphires. I will make your pinnacles of rubies, Your gates of crystal, And all your walls of precious stones. All your children shall be taught by the Lord, and great shall be the peace of your children. In righteousness, you shall be established; You shall be far from oppression, for you shall not fear; and from terror, for it shall not come near you. Indeed they shall surely assemble, but not because of Me. Whoever assembles against you shall fall for your sake. "Behold, I have created the blacksmith. Who blows the coals in the fire, Who brings forth an instrument for his work; and I have created the spoiler to destroy. No weapon formed against you shall prosper. And every tongue which rises against you in judgment You shall condemn. This is the heritage of the servants of the Lord, and their righteousness is from Me," says the Lord.

    Isaiah   54:11-17

Bibliography

India slavery India: The Center of Modern Slavery?https://www.theglobalist.com/india-the-modern-slavery-capital-of-the-world/

Androff, David K. "The Problem of Contemporary Slavery: An International Human Rights Challenge for Social Work." International Social Work 54.2 (2011): 209–22. Print.

Bales, Kevin. "Expendable People: Slavery in the Age of Globalization." Journal of International Affairs 53.2 (2000): 461–84. Print.

Supplementary Convention on the Abolition of Slavery, the Slave Trade, and Institutions and Practices Similar to Slavery, as adopted by a Conference of Plenipotentiaries convened by Economic and Social Council resolution 608(XXI) of 30 April 1956 and done at Geneva on 7 September 1956.

Geordie Rose of Kindred AI presents Super-intelligent Aliens Are Coming to Earth https://www.youtube.com/watch?v=cD8zGnT2n_A

The Philadelphia Inquirer, LLC

800 River Rd, Conshohocken,

PA 19428, United States

Bible: New King James Translation

Scripture taken from the New King James Version®. Copyright © 1982 by Thomas Nelson. Used by permission. All rights reserved.

The Tribune News

National Tribune was an independent newspaper and publishing company owned by the National Tribune Company, formed in 1877 in Washington, D.C. Now public domain in: Historic American Newspapers. Library of Congress.

Michael Jackson, Thriller

Sony Music Entertainment

Ethan Graham

25 Madison Ave,

New York, NY 10010, United States

501©(3)

A 501(c)(3) organization is a corporation, trust, unincorporated association, or other type of organization exempt from federal income tax under section 501(c)(3) of Title 26 of the United States Code. It is one of the 29 types of 501(c) nonprofit organizations in the US. (Wikipedia) https://en.wikipedia.org/wiki/501(c)(3)_organization

Wikimedia Foundation, Inc.

1 Montgomery Street

Suite 1600

San Francisco, CA 94104

USA

Wikipedia text is freely licensed under the Creative Commons Attribution-ShareAlike License (CC-BY-SA),

Saint Patrick

He was the fifth-century Romano-British Christian missionary and bishop in Ireland.

(Wikipedia) https://en.wikipedia.org/wiki/Saint_Patrick

BRICS

acronym coined for an association of five major emerging national economies: Brazil, Russia, India, China and South Africa. Originally the first four were grouped as "BRIC", before the induction of South Africa in 2010.

Founded: June 2006

Formation: 2009

Official language: Portuguese, Russian, Hindi, Chinese, English

Predecessor: BRIC

Leaders: Jair Bolsonaro, Vladimir Putin, Narendra Modi, Xi Jinping, MORE

Founders: China, India, Brazil, Russia

http://infobrics.org/

United Nations

The United Nations is an intergovernmental organization.

Secretary general: António Guterres Trending

Official languages: Arabic; Chinese; English; French; Russian; Spanish;

Founded: October 24, 1945, San Francisco, CA

Headquarters: New York, NY

Subsidiaries: World Health Organization, MORE

(Wikipedia) https://en.wikipedia.org/wiki/United_Nations

Save America: Only Christians Can Do It

CPSIA information can be obtained
at www.ICGtesting.com
Printed in the USA
BVHW070923070421
604343BV00005B/882